LET'S ROCK!

How to Be
a Rock Collector

Natalie Hyde

Crabtree Publishing Company

www.crabtreebooks.com

Crabtree Publishing Company

www.crabtreebooks.com

Author: Natalie Hyde
Publishing plan research and development:
Sean Charlebois, Reagan Miller
Crabtree Publishing Company
Project coordinator: Kathy Middleton
Photo research: Tibor Choleva, Melissa McClellan
Design: Tibor Choleva
Editor: Adrianna Morganelli
Proofreaders: Rachel Stuckey, Crystal Sikkens
Production coordinator: Margaret Amy Salter
Prepress technician: Margaret Amy Salter
Print coordinator: Katherine Berti

Geological consultant:
Callan Bentley, MS, MSSE, Northern Virginia
Community College

Special thanks: Robert Hall Originals,
Sandor Monos

Cover: Rockhound studying a rock (center);
agate stone (left); black lava stones that are
polished smooth by tides (bottom right)

Title page: Close-up view of sea pebbles

This book was produced for Crabtree Publishing
Company by BlueAppleWorks.

Photographs and reproductions:
© dreamstime.com: Pancaketom(headline and boxtop image), Mrreporter (titlepage, 7 middle), Yurchyk(4), Gary Arbach(5), Pancaketom (6 top), Eugene78(6/7 large) Robbiverte (p 8/9 large), Landd09(9 bottom), Yarchyk (10 bottom), Georg Henrik Lehnerer(11 left), Jasonjung(11 right top), Marian Mocanu(11 bottom), Farbled (12 right), Mikhail Markovskiy(14 bottom), Rj Grant(15 middle), Tepyrij(16 top) / © 123rf: designpics(14 bottom), Zelenka68(17 bottom left), Sergey Lavrentev(17 right bottom), Pancaketom (17 large), Simarts(18 bottom), Bruce Riccitelli (25 top right), Clearviewstock (27 middle), Marek Uliasz(27 bottom) / © iStockphoto.com: mikeuk(12top), Terry Wilson(16 bottom), Michael Courtney(18 middle), / © Shutterstock.com: (cover: bottom right and left), Yarchyk (cover: center), Rufous (cover: bottom middle), Jeffrey Schmieg(background every page), beboy(4 bottom), Ivan Coric(5 bottom), Nastya22(6 bottom), DrMadra(left stamp), rook76(middle stamp), IgorGolovniov(right stamp), xpixel(7 top), Stephen VanHorn (8 top), Thomas M Perkins, katatonia82 (8 middle), Seregam(9 top), IRP(9 middle), catherinka (10/11 large), Oleksandr Kostiuchenko(11 top), Gala_Kan(12/13 large), Rufous(12/13 bottom), Boris Mrdja (13 bottom right), bogdan ionescu(15top), Howard Sandler (15 bottom), Luis Santos(17 left top), Elnur (17 bottom right), morrbyte (19 top), Balefire(20/21 large), Muellek Josef(20 left), Kenneth V. Pilon(20 middle), Bill Florence(20 right), Pichugin Dmitry(21 right), Vladi(21 bottom), Artur Bogacki(22 big), Golden Pixels LLC(22 bottom), absolute-india(23 top), bikeriderlondon(25 bottom), chantal de bruijne(26 top), Kenneth V. Pilon(26 middle), markrhiggins(26 bottom), kyokoliberty,(26/27 large), Fedorov Oleksiy(27 top left), goldenangel(27 top right), Dirk Ott(29 bottom left), Nastya22(29 right) / © NASA (19 middle) © Bill Morgenstern (8 bottom right, 23 bottom) / © MMcClellan(14 top, 18 top, 19 bottom, 22 top, 24 all, 25 big, 28 top, 29 top left) / © Lisa Stokes(25 top left)

© David Brock: Illustrations pages 5

Sculpture by Maurice Lund courtesy of Robert Hall Originals, page 28

Library and Archives Canada Cataloguing in Publication

Hyde, Natalie, 1963-
How to be a rock collector / Natalie Hyde.

(Let's rock)
Includes index.
Issued also in electronic formats.
ISBN 978-0-7787-7212-5 (bound).--ISBN 978-0-7787-7217-0 (pbk.)

1. Rocks--Collection and preservation--Juvenile literature.
2. Minerals--Collection and preservation--Juvenile literature.
I. Title. II. Series: Let's rock (St. Catharines, Ont.)

QE433.6.H93 2012   j552.0075   C2012-900248-8

Library of Congress Cataloging-in-Publication Data

CIP available at Library of Congress

Crabtree Publishing Company

www.crabtreebooks.com   1-800-387-7650

Printed in Canada/022012/AV20120110

Published in Canada
Crabtree Publishing
616 Welland Ave.
St. Catharines, Ontario
L2M 5V6

Published in the United States
Crabtree Publishing
PMB 59051
350 Fifth Avenue, 59th Floor
New York, New York 10118

Published in the United Kingdom
Crabtree Publishing
Maritime House
Basin Road North, Hove
BN41 1WR

Published in Australia
Crabtree Publishing
3 Charles Street
Coburg North
VIC 3058

CONTENTS

ROCKY CRUST

Earth's crust is made of rocks that are made of minerals of every shape and color. They are a part of every **landform**, from mountains and plains to caves and the ocean floor.

CYCLING IT!

Earth is constantly renewing itself through the rock cycle. Volcanoes and underwater vents send **molten** rock, or magma, up to the surface. The magma cools and the elements combine to make minerals. The minerals join to make rocks.

▲ Combinations of minerals create many different rocks.

▼ When magma reaches Earth's surface it is called lava.

COOL CHANGE

The cooled magma first forms igneous rocks. Wind, water, and ice break these rocks down into tiny bits called sediment. Sedimentary rock forms wherever these particles gather and build up. When sedimentary rocks are exposed to heat and pressure, such as during mountain building, the structure of the rocks can change. This creates metamorphic rocks.

BUMPY RIDE

The crust of our planet is not just one big piece of rock. The crust is broken into sections called tectonic plates, which are floating on the magma beneath them. The plates are constantly moving and bumping into each other. Mountains are formed when two plates meet and one plate is forced upward. The other plate is pushed downward into Earth's interior, which is very hot. The rock melts into liquid form.

oceanic plate being pushed downward into Earth's core

continental plate pushed up, forming mountains

EXTREME COLLECTION

✳ The Smithsonian's National Gem and Mineral collection has more than 375,000 specimens, including the Hope Diamond and the Star of Asia sapphire.

▼ *The Hope Diamond is set in a special design to celebrate the 50th anniversary of the donation of the Hope Diamond by Harry Winston to the Smithsonian National Museum of Natural History in Washington, DC.*

SHOWING IT OFF

Each part of the rock cycle produces different kinds of rocks and minerals. Many people enjoy finding and displaying the different types, shapes, and colors to create a rock collection.

▼ *The Alps were formed by movements of tectonic plates called regional metamorphism.*

ROCKHOUNDS AND JACKDAWS

The first rock collectors were prospectors looking for valuable minerals and gemstones. Many people now collect all types of rocks and minerals because of their beauty and interesting history.

HOUNDS AND ROCKS

Amateur rock collectors are called rockhounds. They enjoy adding to their collections by taking field trips to search for new **specimens** or by attending rock and mineral shows. Rockhounds may have a small collection of local rocks or a large collection that they add to over many years.

TUMBLE, POLISH, AND SHAPE!

Some rockhounds don't just display their specimens—they like to use their collections to create things. A **lapidary** is an artist who uses minerals or gems to make jewelry or **mosaics**. Lapidaries are skilled at tumbling, polishing, and shaping stones.

IT'S ALL "MINE"

✳ The National Museum in Wales has over 1,000 specimens of coal from all over the world. Coal mining has been an important industry in Wales for centuries.

▲ This rockhound is searching for new specimens.

▼ Earrings made of red jasper

MAKE IT A COMBO

✳ Some collectors combine their passion for stamps and for rocks by making a rock stamp collection. Many countries display the importance of minerals in their country's industry by creating rock stamps.

▼ *Many countries use stamps showing pictures of minerals.*

SPARKLY DOES IT

Some collections feature rocks that are bright and colorful. Jackdaws are collectors that are drawn to shiny, sparkly, or colorful rocks, much like the bird of the same name. These collectors often like to decorate their homes with their stones to show them off.

▶ *Jackdaws are attracted to colorful and shiny objects.*

TAKE IT UP A NOTCH

Some collectors turn their love of rocks and minerals into a career. Petrologists are geologists that study rocks and how they form. Petrologists' collections often end up in universities or museums for others to learn from and enjoy.

▶ *Petrologists often work in remote places.*

ROCK AROUND THE BLOCK!

Rockhounding is a wonderful hobby that does not require a lot of expensive equipment. You can start your collection by simply picking up a rock from your driveway or backyard. But a few basic supplies can make your time spent rock collecting safer and more rewarding.

BOOK A GUIDE

Whether you pick up stones near your home or travel to other sites to find unusual minerals, it is good to have a rock book or field guide to help you identify your discoveries.

▲ A good field guide can be very helpful.

▼ Always wear protective glasses when using a rock hammer.

PICKY HAMMERS

Rock hammers are small tools with a hammer on one side and a pick on the other. Be sure to always wear safety glasses when using a rock hammer. Little shards of flying rock can get into your eyes.

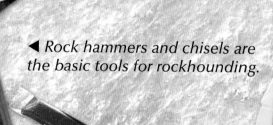

◄ Rock hammers and chisels are the basic tools for rockhounding.

DON'T FORGET THAT TOILET PAPER!

Keep a notebook and pen or pencil with you so you can write down the location of the rocks you find. This is an important part of identifying what you have found. Newspaper or toilet paper is good for wrapping your specimens so they don't get damaged on the trip home. Small plastic or paper bags will keep your rocks separate and allow you to write notes.

BAGGING YOUR ROCKS

A backpack or field bag is a great place to store your supplies, leaving your hands free to explore. Pack a water bottle, sunscreen, bug spray, and a small first aid kit so that you are ready for anything!

▼ *Backpacks are great for storing your supplies and found specimens.*

UP CLOSE

✳ To see small crystals or minerals, use a hand lens to give you a close-up view. It's handy to have one on a **lanyard** around your neck so that you don't have to carry it in your hands.

▼ *Looking at a rock sample using a lens can help with identifying it.*

ainer

GOING PLACES

Rocks are all around us, but not all places are good for rock collecting. Locations where nature exposes new surfaces or moves things around are what most rockhounds look for.

DRY BEDS

Water is one of nature's most powerful forces. It can carve out canyons and move soil and rocks hundreds or even thousands of miles through rushing streams or ocean tides. Dry riverbeds or the banks of flowing rivers are often good places to find unusual specimens.

▶ Bring your best friend with you when rockhounding in dry riverbeds.

▼ Collecting unusual rocks on the beach is always fun!

BEACH ACTION

Beaches are great places to rockhound. The action of the currents and waves can move rocks and minerals long distances. The rocks are often polished and smooth, as they have been bumped and ground along the sandy or rocky bottom.

DO NOT ENTER!

✳ There are some places where rock collecting is NOT allowed: dangerous locations like mines or active **quarries**, provincial or national parks, Aboriginal lands, and private property without permission.

▼ *Obey "No Trespassing" signs when searching for rocks.*

ROCK FACES

Cliff facings or **outcroppings** are good places to find rocks and minerals. These rocks used to be hidden under the ground. As the cliff slowly crumbles, new samples are uncovered. As water, wind, or ice loosens the face, rocks and minerals can fall to the ground below in a pile called a "scree."

▶ *Cliffs and the scree rock below are great places for rockhounding.*

EASY PICKINGS

Abandoned quarries that have been scooped out to mine a certain mineral or ore often expose other rocks and minerals. Heavy equipment has done the hard work of breaking up the rock and makes samples easier to find.

▶ *Broken stones in an abandoned quarry*

ROCK-SOLID CLUES

Identifying the rocks in your collection is a bit like finding clues to solve a mystery. Details like the color, **texture**, and hardness will help you figure out what you have.

WHAT COLOR IS YOUR ROCK?

To get a good look at the color of your specimen, it is sometimes useful to break off a piece so that you have a fresh cut. Using your hand lens, take a close look at whether the rock is light or dark or if there is a mixture of colors.

▶ Breaking a rock can help you identify it.

TEXTURE CLUES

The texture of the rock is also a clue. Because igneous rocks cool slowly, their grains are close together. Sand, mud or gravel particles are often visible in sedimentary rocks. Metamorphic rocks are shaped by heat and pressure, so they are often colored and striped.

▶ Microscopes can be used to identify minerals.

IS IT LIMESTONE?

You will need:

- vinegar
- glass jar or cup
- rocks to be tested

Pour enough vinegar to fill half the cup or jar. Add one rock.

Check for bubbles coming off the rock. Why? Limestone is made of carbonate minerals. When these minerals come in contact with vinegar, there is a chemical reaction that produces carbon dioxide gas, which makes bubbles.

SCRATCH MARKS

Another good clue is the hardness of the rock. Using your fingernail, try to scratch the rock. If it leaves a mark, the mineral is less than a 2 on the Mohs scale of mineral hardness. If it doesn't work try a coin or a steel nail. A mineral scratched by a coin is less than a 3. A mineral scratched by a steel nail is less than 5 ½ on the scale.

NAIL IT!

Now you have enough clues to try to identify your specimen. Using a field guide, compare the color, texture, and hardness to the examples in the book.

▶ *Check that every detail matches the field guide description.*

IDENTIFYING MINERALS

Rocks are made up of minerals such as quartz, mica, and feldspar. Minerals and gemstones can make an interesting collection. Minerals and gemstones are not only identified by color, texture, and hardness, but also by how they break apart, how they shine, and how heavy they are.

TUMBLE IT!

Once you have several rocks and minerals, you will want to clean and organize your collection. A little care and attention as you add specimens will keep your collection at its best.

SHINE AND POLISH

Many rockhounds use a rock tumbler. This machine smoothes and polishes the rough edges of rocks and minerals in much the same way sand and gravel at the bottom of the sea does. Rough rocks are put in the tumbler's barrel with **grit** and water. They bump and grind together until all the sharp edges have worn away.

▲ Rock tumblers come in many different sizes.

▼ Moving water acts like nature's own tumbler. It turns rough stones into smooth pebbles.

YOUR OWN "SEA GLASS"

You will need:

- a rock tumbler
- sand
- petroleum jelly
- water
- broken glass
  (different colors work great)
- thick gloves

Follow the instructions on your tumbler so you do not overload the barrel. Using gloves, carefully add the glass to the barrel. Fill the barrel with water so the level is barely above your glass shards. Add three to four spoonfuls of sand.

Smooth a small amount of petroleum jelly on the outside of the barrel to help it run smoothly. Put the lid on securely and let the tumbler work its magic!

HIDDEN INFORMATION

As your collection grows, it is important to keep track of which rocks and minerals you have and where you found them. Many people use a system of writing a different number on a dried dab of white paint on a hidden spot on each specimen. Then they create a file with file cards, in a notebook, or on a computer. All the information about the rock or mineral is noted beside the number.

▲ White paint works great when you need to mark your minerals.

◄ Tumbled stones and glass pieces are often used to make jewelry.

STORE WITH CARE

As your collection grows, you will need a protected place to store your rocks. A good storage system will keep your specimens from getting mixed up and damaged.

UNDER STRESS

Many specimens are **fragile**. It is best to not handle your collection too much as all minerals can break when they are put under stress. Harder rocks and minerals can grind or break softer ones. Keeping them in a container with separate **compartments** for each specimen is the best idea. This will help keep your collection organized and protected.

▲ Soft, padded containers are great for storing your collection.

▼ Storing rocks on top of each other can cause damage to the softer minerals.

SCRAMBLED ROCKS ANYONE?

Any container with separate compartments will work to store your collection. Egg cartons are handy because they are easy to find and stackable. Plastic embroidery floss containers or tackle boxes will also work.

▲ *Egg cartons have separate compartments that help protect your fragile specimens.*

SUN PROTECTION

It is a good idea to store your collection somewhere dry and out of direct sunlight. Some minerals change color in sunlight. Amethyst and topaz can fade when exposed to light. Some minerals, such as proustite, darken. Other minerals, such as halite, dissolve in water. Halite should not be washed or stored in a damp place.

▼ *Keep topaz out of the light.*

▼ *Keep halites in a dry place.*

HINTS AND TIPS

✳ Make sure your storage container is acid-free. The acid could react with some of your specimens and damage them.

✳ Even though cotton balls are soft, do not use these for fragile specimens. The crystals can get caught in the cotton fibers and break.

✳ Use a soft toothbrush to gently remove bits of mud or dirt.

ROCK SALT

✳ The mineral halite is salt. In its natural form, halite is called rock salt. It is what table salt and road salt are made from. Halite can be found in sedimentary rocks.

SHOWING IT OFF

Making a display of your rocks and minerals is a great way to share your hobby with others. Displays can be big or small and showcase part or all of your collection.

IDENTITY CARDS

There are many ways to display your specimens. A sturdy shelf can hold your favorite examples along with small cards to identify them. Some companies also sell "specimen stands" that hold individual rocks.

THAT GLASSY LOOK

Glass front cabinets are nice because you can see your collection and still protect it from dirt and accidents. You can achieve the same effect by putting specimens in glass jars, tubes, or small bottles. The plastic screw jars, often used to store beads, are also great for rocks because you can see through the side as well as the top. You can also use **magnifying** boxes for very small specimens!

▲ Keep a good duster handy if you plan on storing your collection on open shelves.

▼ If you are putting more than one specimen in a jar, be sure to use rocks with a high hardness level to prevent damage.

OUT OF THIS WORLD!

*Most of the Moon rocks from the Apollo space missions are at the Lyndon B. Johnson Space Center in Houston, Texas. Most are stored in **nitrogen** to keep them dry and are only handled using special tools.

▼ *The most famous of the Moon rocks recovered is the Genesis Rock, which was collected on the Apollo 15 mission.*

THEME SHOW

Some rock displays focus on a certain theme. Rocks and minerals can be grouped by color, size, or location. Different sections of a display can showcase examples of different types of rocks, such as igneous, sedimentary, or metamorphic. Some displays might show different colors and shapes of quartz. Interesting or unusual rocks, such as magnetic, **fluorescent,** or "TV" rocks, also make a fun display.

▼ *A theme display is a great way to show off different samples of the same mineral.*

AMETHYST
Brazil

NATURE SPECIALS

Some rock specimens are formed under certain conditions and can only be found in special places. Such specimens are always a valuable addition to a collection.

UNUSUALLY NATURAL

Natural glass is found in unusual places. When a lightning bolt strikes sand, the temperature is so high that the sand melts and forms long, thin glass structures called fulgurites.

SPACE GLASS

Tektites are a strange natural glass that forms when **meteorites** impact Earth. The incredible heat and pressure from the meteorite melts minerals and shoots them up into the air where they cool as they fall back to Earth as glass.

STONE FOREST

✱ Minerals can also seep into other materials, which creates unusual rocks. When trees fall in the forest, they may be covered with mud and clay over time. Over millions of years, minerals replace the wood under the mud and clay and create a kind of fossil or rock called "petrified" wood.

▼ Petrified wood is a type of fossil. "Petrified" means "turned into a rock."

▼ Moldavite is an olive-green type of tektite that is only found in parts of Eastern Europe.

▼ Indochinite is a tektite that is 700,000 years old.

FOLLOW THE FIREBALL

Scientists estimate that 500 meteorites fall to Earth each year. Some resemble rocks from our own planet, while others are different. Some contain a lot of iron and are very heavy. As meteorites travel through our **atmosphere** they become "shooting stars," and collectors often find them by looking for and following the fireballs.

▼ *The Hoba Meteorite is the largest meteorite ever found and the biggest naturally occurring piece of iron on Earth's surface.*

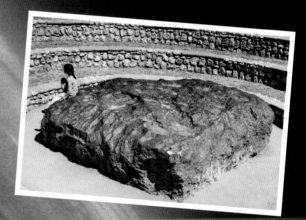

GEE, WHAT ARE THE ODDS?

Geodes are round rock formations that have crystals inside. Sedimentary or igneous rock can form with empty spaces. Water seeps inside and the minerals it leaves behind create crystals. Geodes can be as small as a walnut or large enough to drive into with a truck.

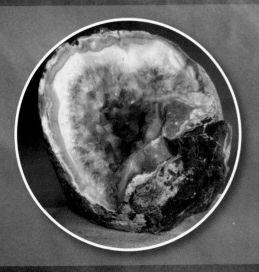

◄ *Crystals are visible inside this amethyst geode.*

JOIN A PACK

It is always fun to share your interest in rock collecting with others. Joining a rock and mineral club is a great way to expand your collection and your knowledge.

HOUND TALK

Meeting with other rockhounds is a good way to share information. People who have been collecting for a long time often have great tips on tools, **techniques**, and locations. Meetings can include **workshops** for trying new activities or guest speakers who share their experiences.

▶ *Mineral specimen samples*

ROCK BADGES

Many clubs encourage younger members by offering sample minerals for beginners. The Future Rockhounds of America have a badge program for junior members. By completing different activities on topics such as meteorites, gold panning, fossils, Earth processes, and leadership, young people can earn 15 different badges.

▶ *Rock collecting with an experienced collector can be very rewarding.*

OUT IN THE FIELDS

Clubs often organize field trips to good collecting sites. Going with a group is not only a lot of fun, it allows you to hunt in locations you might not be able to get to on your own.

IF IN DOUBT, ASK QUESTIONS!

Before joining a club it is a good idea to ask some questions. Find out if there are other young people in the club and if they have a program for kids. If you enjoy hands-on activities or crafts, ask if they offer those opportunities. You should also ask where and how often they go on field trips.

INBOX

✱ Ask an adult to sign you up for a free email newsletter from a rock and mineral club. You can then read up on the latest news and tips about your hobby.

▼ *A newsletter is a good way to stay in touch with other rockhounds.*

▼ *Collecting rocks with your friends can be a lot of fun.*

23

ROCK FAIRS

Rock collectors love nothing better than showing off and sharing their hobby. There are rock, gem, and mineral shows held all over the world.

UNUSUAL AND FASCINATING

Most rock and mineral clubs host a show during the year. This gives their members and the public a chance to see unusual and fascinating specimens. Collectors can also buy and sell rocks and minerals to build their collections.

▲ *Rock collectors love to talk about their collections.*

▼ *Rock sculptors often show off their skills at rock fairs.*

ALL ON DISPLAY

A show will usually have displays of rocks, gems, minerals, crystals, and fossils. There might also be dealers who sell crystals, beads, gemstones, and jewelry supplies. Sometimes shows will have demonstrations of lapidary arts, such as cutting and polishing stones.

▼ *Good fossil specimens can be bought at rock fairs.*

▼ *A turtle carved out of petrified wood*

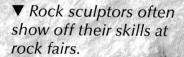

A GEMBOREE

❋ Bancroft, Ontario, is known for its great variety of minerals, especially its large deposits of amethyst. Each year the town hosts a Rockhound Gemboree, which draws thousands of collectors, rockhounds, and geologists. Dealers come from around the world with a huge selection of minerals, gemstones, and lapidary supplies.

▼ *Bancroft's Gemboree is Canada's largest gem and mineral show.*

PRICE CHECK

If you are planning on buying rocks or minerals for your collection at a show, it is a good idea to do some homework before you go. Ask an adult to help you check online for average prices of the size and quality of mineral you want to buy.

IMITATORS

You may also see human-made or synthetic gems and minerals. They are "grown" in laboratories to look just like natural samples.

▼ *Once these synthetic diamonds are cut and polished, they will look just like natural diamonds.*

DIFFERENT? WHY NOT?

Some collectors are interested in more than just rocks and minerals. There are special types of "rock" collecting.

ANCIENT IMPRINTS

Fossil collecting is a branch of rockhounding because fossils are found in and are made of rock. Sedimentary rock is the only type of rock that contains fossils. Some fossils are imprints of ancient plants or animals. Other fossils are minerals that have replaced the original cells of the organism, making a rock **duplicate**.

▲ Many people collect fossils for their beauty and historical value.

SURVIVAL TOOLS

Our ancient ancestors used rocks to make tools and weapons. Arrowheads, harpoon points, scrapers, and hammerstones are all examples of rocks shaped and carved by human hands. These types of rocks make a fascinating collection because they tell the story of how early humans lived and survived.

▶ Stone tools can survive for long periods of time. They provide useful clues about our past.

▲ *Gold nuggets contain pure gold.*

▲ *Pyrite often fools collectors panning for gold.*

GOLD RUSH!

✳ Panning for gold can be a very interesting hobby and takes very little equipment. Just remember that there is a difference between gold and "fool's gold," which is really pyrite!

▼ *Gold nuggets found in gravel can be very small.*

SAND TUBES AND SUCH

Sand collecting is a fun and easy variation of rock collecting. Sand is not just found on beaches; there are sand deposits on mountains, in riverbeds, and even in caves! Sand is made of little particles of rock and minerals and depending on the type of rocks in the area, it can have many different **properties**, such as color.

▶ *Clear test tubes are a great way to display and store your sand collection.*

◀ *Sandstone is a rock made up primarily of sand. Because of this, it is easily **eroded**. Antelope Canyon is located on Navajo land near Page, Arizona. It was formed by the erosion of Navajo Sandstone.*

ROCK CREATIONS

While some people like to display their collections on a shelf or in a case, others like to use their specimens to create things.

NOT FOR WASHING

Soapstone gets its name because it can feel soapy to the touch. It is a metamorphic rock consisting mostly of the soft mineral talc. It can be scratched with a fingernail and has been used for carvings and sculptures for centuries all over the world. The **Inuit** are famous for their soapstone sculptures of whales, seals, and polar bears.

▲ Most soapstone is a shade of gray.

▼ Soapstone carvings often show animals from Arctic regions.

SOUP BOWLS?

Agate is a type of quartz that forms in layers of different colors making a beautifully striped rock. In ancient times it was prized as a **talisman**. Agate can be cut and shaped into bowls or cut into thin slices to be used in stained glass windows.

▼ *Bowls made of agate are unique in appearance.*

▼ *Jewelry made with gemstones is very popular all over the world.*

THAT'S A WRAP!

You will need:

- rock
- craft wire
- wire cutters
- needle-nose pliers
- jewelry cord, string, or yarn

Cut a piece of wire 10 to 12 inches (25 to 30 cm) long. Clamp the tip of the wire with the needle-nose pliers and bend it into a loop large enough for the cord or string to pass through. Wrap the remaining wire around the stone by bending it with your fingers and the pliers. You can wrap it any way you like: spiral, crisscross, or just a creative design. Snip any extra wire with the wire cutters. Bend the cut end toward the stone or under another section of wire so that it will not stick out and scratch. Cut a length of jewelry cord, string, or yarn to fit loosely around your neck and string it through the wire loop to make the necklace.

OH SO POPULAR!

One of the most popular uses for minerals and gemstones is jewelry. **Pendants**, earrings, bracelets, tiaras, and pins are all decorated with many different kinds of rocks, minerals, and even fossils.

GLOSSARY

atmosphere The air or gases surrounding Earth

compartments Separate sections or spaces

duplicate A copy

erode To wear away by water, wind, or ice

fluorescent Glowing; giving off light

fragile Easily broken or damaged

gemstones Valuable minerals used for jewelry

grit Rough particles of sand or stone

Inuit Indigenous peoples of the Arctic

landform Features that make up Earth's surface, such as plains, mountains, and valleys

lanyard A cord worn around the neck for carrying something

lapidary Someone who cuts, polishes, or engraves gems

magnifying Making something appear greater in size

meteorites Rocks that fall to Earth from space

molten Melted

mosaics A picture made of small pieces or tiles set into a surface

nitrogen A colorless, odorless gas in our atmosphere

outcroppings Parts of rock formations that stick out of the ground

pendants An ornament attached to a cord or chain as jewelry

properties Traits or characteristics

prospectors Someone who looks for minerals or gemstones in the ground

quarries Open pits where materials are dug or blasted out of the ground

specimens Samples

synthetic Not natural, human-made

talisman An object thought to have supernatural powers or provide protection

techniques Methods or ways of doing things

texture The roughness or smoothness of a surface

workshops Meetings to learn new skills

MORE INFORMATION

FURTHER READING

Smithsonian Rock and Fossil Hunter.
Morgan, Ben. DK Children, 2005.

Rocks & Minerals.
Morris, Neil. Crabtree Publishing, 1998.

Geology Rocks!: 50 Hands-On Activities to Explore the Earth.
Blobaum, Cindy. Ideals Publications, 2008.

WEBSITES

Rocks for Kids:
www.rocksforkids.com/RFK/collecting.html

Starting a Sand Collection:
www.ajaster.com/Sandbox/Collecting/Collecting.html

Rockhound Kids:
www.rockhoundkids.com/rh-links.html

Future Rockhounds of America
www.amfed.org/kids.htm

The Central Canadian Federation of Mineralogical Societies
www.ccfms.ca/

INDEX